WRITE THROUGH DEPRESSION

LARGE PRINT WORKBOOK EDITION

NATALIE ROBERTS

Write Through Depression: Workbook Edition

First Large Print Paperback Edition (2019)

ISBN-13: 9781091737198

Published by Natalie Roberts
www.natalieroberts.net

Cover Design by: kmwritingdesign.com

For Evan, Abbie, Hannah and Amelia. You can be whatever you want to be.

Work hard and dream big.

I love you!

"Mental pain is less dramatic than physical pain, but it is more common and also more hard to bear. The frequent attempt to conceal mental pain increases the burden: it is easier to say "My tooth is aching" than to say "My heart is broken."

C.S Lewis, The Problem of Pain

CONTENTS

IS THIS BOOK FOR YOU?

If you have picked up this book hoping it will cure your depression, please send it back and get a refund. Also, if you don't like swearing or inspirational quotes then definitely don't read this book. If on the other hand, you love both, keep reading.

Firstly, I'm not a doctor and will never claim to have all the answers. This book is about my personal experience and what worked and still works for me, and it won't apply to everyone. I just want to share what gets me through my depression. It's not one of those books written by someone who's been there, done that, and come through the other side. I am depressed and have been for a long time. But over the years I have found some good coping mechanisms for the really dark times, and I'm so much better than I used to be.

Nothing I say in this book should be taken over professional advice and I'm in no way an expert on depression. I am however, an expert in my own depression. If what I share works for you then that's great. If it doesn't, then it doesn't mean there is something wrong with you or that what I say isn't true.

Everyone is unique and everyone has different coping mechanisms.

Every single person experiences depression differently.

Even if this helps just one person, then I will have achieved what I set out to do.

Most importantly, this book is meant for those who have clinical depression, not those who feel temporarily down or sad because of a short-term situation. There is a huge difference and this book will explain it all.

I hope after all of that you want to carry on reading. If not then I thank you for your time. If you are sticking with me, great! You don't know how much that means to me.

So, let's get into it.

HOW TO USE THIS WORKBOOK

This book is here to be written in, highlighted, drawn on and scribbled all over. Nothing would make me happier than seeing the corner of the pages turned over and notes in the margins.

You do not have to be a master of language, punctuation or grammar to use this book. If your handwriting is terrible - so what? This book is for your eyes only. Spelling mistakes don't matter. Getting what is in your head down on paper does.

Highlight until your heart's content and please send me pictures. This book should not stay in pristine condition!

Fill in the worksheets and make use of the blank pages at the back.

Tweet or upload a picture to Instagram with #WriteThroughDepression and I will see you.

Happy writing!

WHAT IS DEPRESSION?

"If you are going through hell, keep going."

Winston Churchill

Depression is a bitch. It bullies and sucks the life out of you. It destroys relationships, jobs and lives. It grips you around the throat until you feel like you are suffocating. It crushes your chest until you feel you can't breathe anymore, and then it leaves you for dead.

Nice isn't it!

People are dying from depression every day. It infects you like a disease and you deteriorate until you don't recognise yourself. But it doesn't have to be that way. You can take control of it. To do this you need to acknowledge how you feel and ask for help.

I know, you don't like asking for help do you? It makes you weak doesn't it?

NO, IT DOES NOT!

Asking for help is the strongest and bravest thing someone can do. Suffering in silence never helped anyone, and it certainly didn't change their life or make them happy. It's okay to be vulnerable.

But what actually is depression?

I'm not going to tell you anything very medical or technical as I'm not an expert. I'm going to explain what I think it is and what research, talking to professionals and listening to others with depression has taught me.

I know it's a serious medical condition and should be treated as such. It's more than feeling down for a few days or because of a temporary situation. It affects all aspects of your life, from work to personal relationships. It's a chronic condition, but it CAN be treated. Treatment doesn't always mean taking medication either, so don't be put off by the thought of pills. But again, for treatment to happen you have to recognise and acknowledge that something isn't right.

You might not know that the signs and symptoms you are experiencing are depression. You might think that everyone feels the same as you and that the way you are feeling is just life. If you are regularly feeling low, sad or miserable throughout the day, and it lasts a few weeks at a time then you might have depression. A doctor can diagnose you, so it's really important to make an appointment if the feelings are lasting for a prolonged period of time, or if they re-occur on a regular basis.

Everyone feels low or down from time to time, but it is important to differentiate this from constant negative self-talk and feelings.

Types of depression

There are many different types of depression. Examples can include:

Major Depressive Disorder (MDD) - This is said to be the most common. The main symptom is a continued depressive mood which lasts more than two weeks. The depression affects all aspects of life including, jobs, family life and other relationships. This is what I have.

Dysthymia - Similar to MDD. It's a more chronic form of depression that lasts longer than two years.

Bipolar Disorder - This is considered a mood disorder. Depression is a symptom of bipolar disorder not a form of depression in itself. Bipolar is categorised by changes in mood from mania to depression.

Seasonal Affective Disorder (SAD) - Similar to MDD, but it only occurs at a certain time of year. Usually winter when the days are shorter and it gets darker earlier.

Prenatal/Antenatal Depression - This is less talked about than postnatal depression, but that is starting to change. It has the same signs and symptoms as other types of depression such as, suicidal thoughts, feeling worthless and losing interest in sex. Just because someone is pregnant it doesn't mean they are happy. It's important to get help straight away, otherwise it's likely to carry on postnatally.

Women can feel pressurised to feel happy and grateful during pregnancy. Because of this they often hide how they feel and this is the same for post-natal and other forms of depression. Depression can affect the baby so getting help is extremely important.

I've had prenatal and postnatal depression so don't feel embarrassed or alone. Just because it's not spoken about doesn't mean it's not happening to lots of other mothers.

Postnatal/Postpartum Depression

Hormones can trigger depression in women who have just given birth. Oestrogen and progesterone increase rapidly in the first twenty-four hours after giving birth. They can then quickly drop, which is thought to cause an imbalance that can lead to depression. Add this to the fact your whole life has changed, you're sleep deprived and a tiny human is totally dependent on you, and it's not hard to see how mums can become depressed.

I speak more about my prenatal and postnatal depression in the 'My Story' section of this book.

What can cause depression?

Many different things can cause depression and some have been explained above, but usually it's a combination of several factors. Some of these include:

•Bereavement

•Bullying

•Loss of a job/ money worries

•End of a relationship

• Pregnancy and birth

• Substance abuse

• A traumatic event

• Medical conditions - Chronic pain, terminal illness, head injury and others

• Certain medications

• Family history / genetics

• Change in season

• Personality - Low self-esteem / self-critical

• A combination of any of the above

This list is not exhaustive.

Everyone's depression and what causes it will be different, but some of the feelings we experience can be similar.

Here are a few ways I've heard people describe what depression feels like:

• It's like wading through treacle

• Drowning but no one can see or hear you

• Can only see the bad in the beautiful

• Like someone constantly flicking a switch on and off

• Existing not living! (This one resonates with me the most)

• Empty/hollow

• I'm a waste of a person

• Everything seems pointless

• Everyone hates me

• I'm not worth it/ I'm not important

• One minute you can run the world, the next you feel stupid and embarrassed

• Constantly exhausted even when you've done nothing to feel that way

• Look at other people and wonder what it's like to be happy

• Look at other people and wonder how they are so motivated and get shit done

• Things will always be the same. Nothing will ever be any better

• I fail at everything I do, so why bother trying

• I don't know why anyone would love me

Do any of these sound familiar? **Y/N**

Write here how you would describe YOUR depression. If you are not sure, come back to this at the end of the book:

....

....

....

....

....

....

....

....

I've written a few signs and symptoms I experienced and were pointed out to me by others, that ultimately made me realise everything was not 'normal' or okay.

Signs and symptoms of depression can include but are not limited to the following. Highlight any you are experiencing right now:

Tearful

Self-harm

Feeling helpless

Guilt

No motivation

Difficulty making decisions

Anxious

Intolerant

Loss of appetite

Suicidal

Feeling hopeless

Irritable

Sad

Constant low mood

Make rash decisions

Lethargic

Poor memory

Poor concentration

Isolating self

Sleeping a lot

Unable to sleep

•   •   •

You don't have to have all of these. Some of these symptoms can be signs of other conditions so always consult a doctor, and you may also have different signs and symptoms.

Here are some more common negative feelings that you may be experiencing.

Highlight the five you are feeling the most:

Ashamed

Lonely

Overwhelmed

Worthless

Disrespected

Manipulated

Trapped

Misunderstood

Rejected

Unloved

Lied To

Defensive

Violated

Cynical

Uninteresting

Miserable

No good

Unworthy

Write any other feelings you are experiencing if they are not listed:

....

....

....

....

....

....

....

....

Now we are going to do something you might feel uncomfortable with or struggle to do.

Highlight at least five positive emotions you feel or

want to feel. Use different colours for ones you feel and the ones you want to feel:

Intelligent

Motivated

Joy

Happy

Gratitude

Strong

Loved

Independent

Hopeful

Cared For

Confident

Determined

Needed

Lucky

Courage

Write any positive emotions you feel here if they are

not listed:

....

....

....

....

Did you find it difficult to highlight five positive emotions? **Y/N**. If yes, write why:

....

....

....

....

....

What can you take away from this chapter that will help you?

....

....

....

....

2

MY STORY

"A word after a word is power."

Margaret Atwood

I have depression it doesn't have me!

Some people think you shouldn't talk about depression. I saw a post on Twitter recently where an author posted a picture, and the caption was something along the lines of 'don't tweet you are depressed, sad or angry because trolls will target you.' There is a good argument for what she said, because trolls are disgusting and will target the vulnerable, but for me personally, that is bullshit. I don't mind talking about it or tweeting about it. I want other people to know they are not alone and it comforts me when other people openly talk about it. I can only be a target if I let myself be one. I retweet a lot of self-help and depression posts. I interact with people who have depression and openly talk about it. I also recently changed my university degree. I was studying a humanities course, but decided a mental health course was more suited to my life and future ambitions. It's also another way for me to take control of my depression.

"No one can make you feel inferior without your consent."

Eleanor Roosevelt

I may be depressed, but I'm not weak when it comes to sticking up for myself. I don't let people walk all over me and that's how it will always be. What I think about myself and what I allow other people to say or do to me are two different things.

"What people think of me is none of my business."

Wayne Dyer

Someone I get strength from and follow a lot on social media is Matt Haig. He wrote Reasons to Stay Alive and this book has been a great help to me and many others. He tweets and posts on Facebook about depression regularly. He's not afraid to talk about it and stand up for people with depression. Ruby Wax and Stephen Fry are also well known for talking about their depression.

* * *

Depression has been in my life since I was 15. Well, that's when I can pinpoint a change in me. It may have happened sooner, but I was too young to remember or realise if it did. If I'm honest, up until 2018, I don't remember a time when I felt truly happy. I would look at other people and wonder what it must feel like to be truly happy. To want to get out of bed and go out. To have motivation and drive. If you are reading this book, because I actually got around to finishing and publishing it, then you are holding a miracle in your hands. Motivation has never come easily to me, but now my mindset is focused more on the positive, so I accomplish more. My mindset change and more positive outlook is down to the people I surround myself with now.

They say what doesn't kill you makes you stronger. Eventually that may be true, but initially what doesn't kill you will leave you weak and wounded and it's a slow process to recovery. Fully recovering may never be possible, but that's okay.

• • •

My early life

My household was not a happy one growing up. Huge arguments between my parents were an everyday occurrence. I should say I was never physically hurt. However, bruises heal, emotional shit stays with you for life. What happens to you and what you witness as a child will shape how you are as an adult, no matter how much you try and stop it. But it doesn't have to dictate how you live your adult life. This is something I learned recently. It's taken me until I'm in my thirties to realise this.

My mum is the strongest person I know - now. I say now, because as a child I thought she was weak. Being an adult and knowing what I know now, I shouldn't have thought that at all. Abuse, like depression, changes you as a person. When you are gripped by fear you act out of character, and I know that now. For a child. the world is black and white. You look up to your mum, and when you think she's letting you down it hurts.

Mum, you didn't let me down. Eventually you found strength, and I'm glad you did because your life is so much better now. In a way, you showed me what I didn't want for my children and for myself, and I have made sure I will never be disrespected or abused. I wish you hadn't gone through everything you did, but I think you are a better person for it now. It's because of you, me and my sister take no shit!

My first bad childhood memory is of my mum being hit. I was around four years old and I remember hiding behind the sofa. You may be thinking why is she talking about abuse when this is a book about depression? Well, think about a child witnessing their mum being hit. This is something they will always remember and carry into adulthood. I believe witnessing physical and emotional abuse had contributed significantly to why I have depression. I've lost count of the times we fled the house late at night. My mum would pack a bag for us and drive down the back roads where we lived. We would stay there for a few hours, but I knew we would have to go back. She had to take us back. We had nowhere else to go. And so, the cycle continued.

My dad was never bad to me. I spent a lot of time with him as a child. I went to work with him and he always bought me what I wanted and gave me money. I think paying me off made him feel better. But no matter how nice he was to me, the way he treated my mum made me hate him. As of 2019, I've not seen or spoken to him for over 14 years. He doesn't live far away and my sister sees him on a regular basis, but I don't, and I'm not upset about it. He's never properly met any of my children. The two older know him as my sister's dad, and they have spoken to him at parties, as he is a children's entertainer. He will probably never meet my youngest babies and I think it's for the best. Some things you can't forgive. I know many people have lost their dad and would give anything to have them back. I'm sorry for this, but just because someone is alive, whether they are your parent or not, it doesn't mean you have to have contact with them.

I'm happy that my sister has both a mum and dad in her life. I can honestly say I've never felt jealous that she has a relationship with her dad, because I feel better off not being in contact with him. I've seen the worst of what a toxic relationship can look like, and some things can't be forgiven. I don't think about him on a day-to-day basis. When someone talks about their dad or my kids talk about theirs, my brain doesn't register that I have one too. When the relationship with my husband broke down (more on this later) I tried my hardest to be civil for the sake of the kids, and he did to. Luckily we get on well now and agree on how to parent the kids. He's a very hands on dad and I'm happy my older two kids have him. I want my kids to look back and be proud we get on.

* * *

Up until I was eight I loved school. Playing house

with my friends, being the teacher's pet and drinking milk out of a glass bottle at break time (yes I'm that old now). Memories I will treasure forever. When I was eight, I moved from infants to juniors (kindergarten to elementary) and that's when it all went downhill. I'm a highly sensitive person. I will never show someone they have hurt me but the smallest comment, even if it's a joke will affect me for days. I will analyse and think about it all day and night until I feel more shit than I should.

One day at school we were taking a spelling test. I remember it like it was yesterday. The test began and I noticed the girl sitting next to me was looking over. In school, we all sat at the same table, so it was easy for someone to look over. I didn't really know why she was looking at my paper because being honest I wasn't the best pupil. She kept looking over for a long time but the teacher didn't notice. I tried to cover the paper with my arm and as I did I looked over at the girl and the teacher saw me. She shouted at me, took me away from the table and made me take the test outside the class room. It upset me so much. I told my mum, and then I quickly refused to go back to the school ever again. I'm sure my mum thought I was being a drama queen at first, but she soon realised every morning when she got screaming, shouting and tears from me that it wasn't a joke. Being accused of cheating by that teacher and her not listening to my explanation deeply affected me. In the end, my mum had to move me to another school because it got that bad.

It happened again in my adult life. A few years ago, I was completing an assignment for a diploma in health and social care. I was a carer in a nursing home at the time and had to write a reflective account of an incident that occurred. I needed to get it signed by the nurse who had been with me for evidence. The nurse read it and accused me of not writing it myself.

Now, for any writer something like that cuts deep. Already being highly sensitive to criticism this really upset me. My assessor knew I had written it, but the fact someone would question my integrity really affected me. I'm sure the nurse in question didn't really think about what she was saying but even today it bothers me. For most people, something like that would probably annoy them and make them angry, but they would let it go, eventually. For me that will be with me for life and I lost respect for the nurse in question and made sure she never read or signed anything to do with my qualifications again.

It's not only when it happens to me either. If I see someone else being questioned, bullied or humiliated I take it personally. I can't help it. I wish I could. I was always taught to stick up for myself and other people and when they are hurt it hurts me too.

If you ask people about me they may say my personality is quite hard and I come across as a snob. These would only be people who don't know me well and I come across that way to protect myself. For anyone who does know me well I would hope they would say I'm kind, caring and too sensitive for my own good.

I don't really care what people who don't know me think, because I don't live my life by their opinion. I care what my loved ones think and that's the most important thing to me. That's not to say I would do what they tell me. I consider what they say and how something I do will affect them before I do it, but I won't let them stop me if it's what I really want. At the end of the day it's my life and I would never tell them what to do with theirs.

When I was 15 I decided I wasn't going to school anymore. There was no rhyme or reason for my decision, but I dug my heels in and decided I wasn't going no matter what anyone said. These days in the UK, my mum could face prison for it, but luckily that was not the case back in 2000/2001. Plus, I went to a private school, so there were different rules. Yes, I said private school. Anyone who knows me laughs at this. I'm far from private school material and truly it didn't do me any good. I wasn't sporty or musical and that's what was favoured in the school I went to, and my family were not rich. I was there on a partial scholarship, and my mum had to work three jobs to send me, which meant there was no money for anything else. Add that to a school full of rich friends and it didn't mix well. I want to point out that no one ever treated me differently and like I was 'poor'. We were not 'poor', but in comparison we had little money. The friends I made in private school were good ones and I love seeing what they are all doing now.

Mum took me to the doctor and he tried to make me see a counsellor. Of course, I refused because at 15 I knew it all. This was the worst year for me to refuse to go to school. It was my GCSE year. For those unfamiliar with GCSE's, they are examinations you take age 15-16 at the end of year 11, and depending on your grades, you use them to get into further education. I refused to revise and in the end came out with four GSCE's. Usually students aim for no less than five GCSE's, grades A-C, and that's what most further education facilities looks for from applicants. I was surprised I got any to be honest and so was my mum. I've made up for it now and have lots of qualifications, mainly in health and social care. I do like to do things the hard way. Education is extremely important to me, but I don't put a lot of value in exams. Everyone learns differently. I'm better when my qualifications are work-based. There is too much pressure on children to get the grades!

Can you see a pattern?

I didn't care about myself, my education or my future and it started from the age of 15 or maybe even eight.

I've never been able to stick at anything. I've had lots of jobs and the longest I've stuck at one was being a carer and that lasted six years, give or take. I put that down to my mum being my boss and not wanting to let her down. I start things and never finish most of the time. I tell people I will go out and do things with them. We make plans and when it comes to the day I make excuses because I don't want to leave the house.

I'm not going to lie to you. I said at the beginning of this book that I'm not someone who's overcome depression. I'm just someone who's found ways to cope through the dark days and I want to share my strategies, in the hope that it will help someone else. Some days are a struggle just to shower. I find that I start bargaining with myself. If I have a shower and do the day-to-day chores then I can go back to bed. I get my grocery shopping purposely delivered at a time that will force me to get out of bed and dressed. Once I'm up, I stay up and get shit done, but to actually move I make deals with myself. This isn't every day, but it happens regularly. Less so now have a toddler for obvious reasons. Some of you may be reading this thinking, big deal, you got up and put your shopping away and to you I say, you don't truly understand depression if you think this. To me it's an achievement. It may be a small one to some, but it feels like a big one to me when I'm having a particularly bad day. I could easily stay in bed feeling like I'm physically and mentally rotting away.

Does any of this sound like you? **Y/N**

What resonates with you the most and why?

....

....

....

....

....

....

....

....

....

• • •

Did you bargain with yourself today or have you in the past? **Y/N**

If yes, what were the terms and what was the outcome?

....

....

....

....

....

Are you holding on to a bad memory from your childhood that you want to let go of? If yes, what is it?

....

....

....

....

....

....

....

....

. . .

Accept what you can't change and move on. The past has gone.

Becoming an adult

I left home when I was 19, mainly to get away from the arguing. I couldn't wait to leave and as soon as the opportunity arose, I was gone. I moved in with my boyfriend who was later to become my husband and two years later and after moving house three times I became pregnant.

I got married when I was 21. This is relatively young these days. I never thought I would get married or have kids. I think what I had witnessed in my childhood put me off. But when I met my now ex-husband (more on this later), I changed my mind. We got married after being together for two and a half years. I had already had my first child by then.

Pregnancy

I really enjoyed being pregnant and it gave me something to focus on with my first two children. My third pregnancy was a lot harder and there were lots of problems throughout and I'm not ashamed to say that most of the time I hated being pregnant. I'm pregnant again with my fourth child as a write this and so far due to medical issues it's not been easy, and it's taken its toll on my body, now I'm older.

Even though I enjoyed the first two pregnancies, how I felt about myself got worse. I believe I had post-natal depression, but I was never diagnosed with it because I didn't ask for help. I suffered in silence, telling people I was fine when I clearly wasn't. My husband and mum could see this, but you can't make someone get help if they don't want to. I felt helpless, worthless and stupid. It was a chore to do anything. I had to be forced out of the house. Once I was out I had a nice time but every time it was an argument to get me to go. When someone offered to take my child, even for 15 minutes, I was relieved and grateful.

The same happened when I had my second child, but the pressure of two kids made everything a million times worse. I didn't get dressed unless I had to. I left the house at the very last minute to pick up my son from school, so I didn't have to socialise with the other parents at the school gate.

When my husband was off he had to do everything. Cooking, cleaning and looking after the kids. I liter-ally switched off and pretended they didn't exist.

I was irritable and lost my temper at the slightest

thing. All I thought about was sleeping. If someone disturbed me there was hell to pay. I ate nothing but junk food and hated looking at myself in the mirror. In the summer, I would put a towel over the bathroom window to block out the light, so when I looked in the mirror it was dark and I could just see enough to put my makeup on. I never opened the blinds or curtain and if someone did open them it would irritate me. I wanted to stay in the dark. I think this is a powerful reflection of how I was feeling.

I often felt like my kids would be better off without me. What good is an irritated, short- tempered depressed mum to a child? At least that's what I thought anyway. I now feel like my kids are mine for a reason. I gave birth to them for a reason. I've literally had nights when I've prayed they never turn out like me and I'm agnostic. I wanted them to be everything I'm not. But recently I've come to realise that I'm not all bad. There are parts of me I want them to inherit, and I want them to learn from me. The main one being sticking up for themselves and others.

Jobs, houses and material things are of no concern to me. I do tell them regularly that if they want nice things and want to travel and have no money worries then they need to work hard in school and life. But deep down all I care about is that they are happy. I couldn't care less what job they have, who they love or what they believe as long as happiness is number one.

Most of my married life we were in debt. A year before we split up we went debt free, but when we split we both had to get loans to survive, thus throwing us back into the debt we had worked hard to get out of. Debt can destroy relationships and it was a factor, albeit not the main factor in our separation.

2008 was one of the lowest points and we eventually asked for help from a debt charity. We had to use a food bank to eat. We lived in disgusting social housing and were far from happy. I then got pregnant with my first daughter and not long after that my then husband was diagnosed with skin cancer. He was okay in the end, but it was a scary time. He was only 32 when he was diagnosed.

When I write it all down like this, I can see how I was depressed. But there is always going to be some sort of shit happening to you. I've now realised it's how you deal with it that can change your life. Mindset is so important. Wallowing and feeling sorry for yourself is perfectly normal. What's not normal is letting the bad shit take over your life until you can't function anymore or you think dying would be a better option.

DYING IS NEVER AN OPTION!

Separation

We went through a lot in our marriage and I think that's why we have ultimately stayed friends, but in 2015 my marriage fell apart after nearly 12 years of being together. I know he won't mind me saying, but from a few years into the marriage we became more best friends than husband and wife. I'm not going to go into the personal details because some things should be private, but I blame myself for how it turned out. He put up with me being moody, irritable and depressed for many years and in the end it was me, not him that ended the relationship. I met someone else and I'm not and never will be proud of everything that happened after that.

In October 2015, I went through what I believe to be a manic period. I didn't care what I was doing or who I was hurting. I couldn't understand why everyone was going on at me when I was happy. I felt like everyone was against me and didn't want me to be happy. This is of course a sign of mania and I can see that now. When you are on a high the only way to go is down and in the November I crashed and burned, but not before spending up a storm and getting myself into more debt again. I was crying every day and it got so bad I went to the doctor for help, something I had always said I would never do. I thought it was a sign of weakness to ask for help, but I was so wrong. It's a sign of great strength when you can admit you can't cope and need help. I always wanted to be seen as a strong person. I wanted people to say I was the strongest person they knew. I thought that admitting I couldn't cope was the opposite of this. I was wrong again!

I was put on antidepressants straight away. I love my doctor. We have a great relationship, and he genuinely cares about me. I already knew him through working in the care home and he would always go out of his way to check on me when he visited the home. The anti-depressants helped control my anger. I had been very angry since my relationship boke down, but they didn't help how I felt. No matter what dose I took, I saw no difference and neither did my family. I was offered counselling but I never took it up. I regret this now. I think it would have helped me a lot, but at the time just telling the doctor I needed help was all I could manage.

I want to be clear that just because they didn't work for me, it doesn't mean they won't for you and you NEED to try them before ruling it out. I know many people, family and friends included, who they have helped and continue to help.

I don't know why they didn't work for me, but personally I found talking to my friends and writing helped me more. My friends' support helped me more than they will ever know. They never treated me like I was ill, they just treated me like Natalie, and that helped me immensely.

Other relationships

I've never had many friends and being honest that's the way I prefer it. It's about the quality not the quantity, and I say this to my kids all the time. I have three close friends that I can tell anything to and although I wouldn't say I'm extremely close emotionally to my mum, I can still tell her anything.

I've always found it hard to accept love from partners, and my children. I don't feel worthy. But on the other hand, I won't be treated badly or disrespected, so deep down I must have some respect and love for myself. The brain is a dangerous thing when you are not in control of it. Being this way can cause problems in my relationships. Partners have thought I didn't love them anymore or want to be in a relationship, when really it was about how I felt about myself, not how I felt about them. It still affects relationships now and my better half can get quite upset about it. I just feel really uncomfortable, but I do try. I have to go to them, if they come to me I automatically shut down. I'm not sure this will ever change. Public displays of affection are a definite no. I will hold hands but that's as far as it goes and if I see other people displaying PDA I get really uncomfortable. I'm not used to affection. My mum will be the first to admit she's the same. I don't remember hugging my mum. We are close in our own way and I can talk to her about anything but we are not a touchy-feely family. I try to be different with my kids. I kiss them, cuddle them and tell them I love them. But when I do, it sometimes feels strange. I don't know why I feel like that. I love doing it but my brain likes to remind me that I'm not used to displays of affection.

As a child, I didn't witness love or affection between my parents. It wasn't until my sister was born when I was 12, that I began to witness affection. I think my mum wanted it to be different for my sister and they are a lot closer than we were. My sister and I show each other affection by making fun of each other. I'm a very sarcastic person and appreciate others who are the same.

* * *

Please, if you only take one thing away from this book then let it be talking to someone. Doctor, family, friend or counsellor. Anyone who will listen and not judge. You will soon see you are not alone. Like with anything, once you talk about it you will find that more people than you realise will be or will have experienced what you are going through. I know women find it easier to talk than men do. Society tells men that showing their feelings is weak and not manly. I say this is bullshit.

If you are a man have you asked for help? If not, why?

....

....

....

....

....

....

....

If you are a pregnant woman or have just given birth and haven't asked for help, what's stopping you? What do you fear?

....

....

....

....

....

. . .

If like me you find affection difficult, why do you think this is?

....

....

....

....

....

....

....

How do you like to be shown affection?

....

....

....

....

....

....

....

. . .

How do you show affection?

....

....

....

....

....

....

....

What can you take away from this chapter that will help you?

....

....

....

....

....

....

It's your turn to let it all out, and dig deeper in the next chapter.

3

YOUR STORY

ISN'T OVER YET!

"Never too old, never too bad, never too late, never too sick to start from scratch once again."

Bikram Choudhury

So now I've told my story, it's your turn. You are the author of your own life. You create the storyline, and you decide how it progresses and changes. My story was something I wasn't happy with, so I started re-writing it. Think of your life as a series of books rather than a standalone novel. It can progress, change and develop how you please. Would you be happy to let someone you love read the story of your life so far? If the answer is no, then it's time for a rewrite.

These questions are ones I've asked myself many times. I found it helped to write them down and see it in black and white. Answer them as honestly as you can. Being honest with yourself is really important. Honesty gives you control. If you continue to lie to yourself, you can't change the way you feel. You will never know what you really want if you keep lying. If you have lied to yourself because you worry what others will think of you, then you are giving them too much power. You are basing your life on the fact you think you have to be a certain way, or different to please others. Never change who you are or what you think to please others. They won't care.

How do you feel right now?

....

....

....

....

....

....

• • •

When did your depression start? Do you even know? Write here when you think it did:

....

....

....

....

....

....

What was the trigger? You can write more than one if you believe many things contributed to it.

....

....

....

....

....

....

Have you asked for help?

....

....

....

....

....

....

....

....

If you have asked for help who did you ask and why?

....

....

....

....

....

....

....

If you haven't asked for help why haven't you?

What's stopping you?

....

....

....

....

....

....

....

Is depression affecting your relationships? If so how?

....

....

....

....

....

....

....

Is it affecting your work? How?

....

....

....

....

....

....

....

....

Are you dependent on someone? (Emotionally / financially or both)

....

....

....

....

....

....

....

. . .

If you are dependent on someone what could you do to ensure it doesn't carry on? This probably isn't going to happen quickly. It may take a while to answer this. You can come back to it, but don't leave it for too long:

....

....

....

....

....

....

....

....

Are you in debt? If so what's the total amount? Write each debt, amount owed and total debt overall.

This can be a bit of a shock when you write it down, but it's important to know so you can take control and make a plan. Debt has contributed a lot to my depression, and it wasn't until I took action, that I began to feel more in control:

....

....

....

....

....

....

....

....

Name something you have achieved that you are proud of:

....

....

....

....

....

....

....

• • •

What's the one thing in your life you want to change the most?

....

....

....

....

....

....

....

What are you good at?

....

....

....

....

....

....

....

What are your goals in life?

I know it's hard to think about these when you are depressed, but without any it will be hard to move forward. Everyone has dreams. Mine was to be a published author. They don't have to be huge goals. Start with small, realistic ones:

....

....

....

....

....

....

....

....

What are your personal goals? Mine were and still are, spending more time with my children and being kinder to myself:

....

....

....

....

....

....

....

....

What do you think are your five best traits?

....

....

....

....

....

What do you think are your five worst traits?

....

....

....

....

....

•　•　•

Name a time when you have felt helpful to someone and why:

....

....

....

....

....

....

How do you feel after answering these questions? Be honest.

....

....

....

....

....

....

....

....

•   •   •

What can you take away from this chapter that will help you?

....

....

....

....

....

....

....

....

....

....

....

....

....

....

....

4

START WRITING NOW

"Write what disturbs you, what you fear, what you have not been willing to speak about. Be willing to split open."

Natalie Goldberg

I have found one of the best ways to deal with, and control my depression is to write. Write my thoughts, feelings and fears unedited. You're probably thinking, well that's her job; I'm not a writer. You're right it is my job, but it hasn't always been. Long before I got any book deals or articles published, I was writing in journals. You don't need to be a professional writer or even particularly good at writing at all, as I explain at the beginning of this book. Like the saying goes 'dance like no one is watching,' well you can write like no one is reading.

I'm a firm believer in talking to people and talking helped me, but it has always been edited up to a point. I'm careful what I say especially to friends and family. I don't want to upset them, or make them worry even more than they do already. So, I started writing in a journal. It doesn't have to be an expensive journal. It can be a cheap notebook or even some paper folded over to look like a book. If you love all things digital then make a folder on your desktop or download a notes app onto your mobile device.

If you have been filling in the questions in this book, hopefully it has inspired you to carry on writing. They were trigger questions to get you thinking about your habits, and if they are contributing to your depression. You will probably find they do. You may already feel relief at letting some of it out. If you don't then it doesn't mean writing isn't for you. It just means we haven't asked the right questions or found the right medium for you yet.

Author Joan Didion said, *"I don't know what I think until I write it down."*

I write to understand what I feel about something. Writing isn't necessarily going to 'cure' your depression. But it can really help keep you in control. I like to write about how I'm feeling, what's making me feel that way, and all the deep dark thoughts I wouldn't tell anyone. I like to finish it off on a positive note. Sometimes I have to force myself to do it, but I write at least one thing I'm grateful for at the end of each journal entry.

Write something you are grateful for today here:

....

....

....

....

....

....

....

....

If you skipped over the last question because you couldn't think of anything you are grateful for today, then try again. It can be something as simple as your cup of tea tasted great today, it wasn't raining or you got your kids to school on time; you can see where I'm going with this.

There are lots of ways you can express your thoughts and feelings through writing. Not all types of writing will be suitable for everyone, but more than one way to express yourself may be helpful.

Journaling

This is my number one favourite method of expressing my feelings.

I have two journals. One for my negative thoughts and one for my business and creativity. If I don't feel like I've done something creative every day, it makes me feel down. Writing in the journal is creative and expressive, so it fills that need inside me.

Depression is overwhelming and confusing. Thoughts become jumbled and making sense of life and situations you find yourself in can be overwhelming. When your mind starts to race it can be scary and upsetting. Trying to understand it all can be difficult. This is when writing and journaling can help. Getting the thoughts out of your mind and onto paper can be freeing. Don't worry if you think you are not good at writing. The journal is for your eyes only, unless you decide to share it with someone. Spelling and grammar aren't important, but releasing your thoughts on to the paper is.

Talking to a therapist, as I mentioned before is also a

good tool but it is usually edited up to a point, for fear of embarrassment and rejection. Writing your thoughts and emotions down unedited is a great way to understand how you are feeling, without fear of judgement or ridicule. Journaling allows you to be yourself, and enables you to express how you feel in the rawest form.

There are other great reasons you should start journaling, and here are a few:

Getting to know yourself

How many of us really know ourselves in the true sense? You may be surprised by what you learn about yourself when you start writing. Many people find out they are more resilient than they thought. Some realise they are highly sensitive, and others may find that they complain a lot rather than showing gratitude. However, in the midst of depression, complaining and feeling sorry for yourself is common and those feelings are hard to control.

Seeing it all written down may be the realisation you need to find out something positive or negative about yourself. It could be the trigger that helps you change your behaviour.

Symptom Tracking

If you are writing in a journal on a regular basis you should soon see a pattern emerge. Looking back on particularly bad days you may find you have the same triggers or situations that make you feel worse about yourself.

Monitoring your symptoms can be extremely useful for recovery.

Things you can write about include:

- Your symptoms
- The time of day your mood changed
- Stress factors that may have contributed to the mood change
- The severity of your symptoms (mild, moderate or severe)
- What relieved these symptoms, if anything?

Tracking in this way can show you what to avoid or change and can also be good for showing you what calms you down and relieves your symptoms. You need to be writing consistently to see a pattern emerge.

Problem Solving

Releasing your problems and concerns onto the page can also help you come up with solutions. Writing gives you time to think through your problems. Writing them down and being able to see them can help you prioritise and decide which problem to tackle first.

You should write down:

- What is your problem?
- Why is this problem bothering you in particular? Be in-depth about the reasons it's upsetting you or making you worry.
- Is there a certain person that is affecting how you feel?

You can then start to think about, and write down possible solutions to your problems. What steps do you need to take and can anyone help you? You may also identify future problems that might occur and you can prevent them from happening.

Finally make a plan on how you will achieve what you need to do, and start to work on sorting out the problem.

How to Start Journaling

The first thing you need to think about is the purpose of your journal. When you know the purpose, you can choose how and when to do it. If you are full of negativity, then a gratitude journal may be for you. If you are craving creativity, then consider releasing your feelings through an art journal.

There are many different ways to journal, you just need to choose the best for you.

1. *Daily Journal* – This is like a diary. You write in it daily or weekly if you are short for time. It is a record of your day/week. Who did you see? What connections did you make? What went well and what didn't go well? And so on. Write about how your day/week went and the thoughts and feelings you had.

2. *Problem Solving Journal* – This journal is solely to record your problems, and finding ways to solve them in a productive and positive way. It's not specifically for day-to-day. You can write in it whenever a problem pops up that you think is making you depressed.

Write what the problem is and why it's concerning/causing you trouble. Then write what measures you are going to take to overcome it. It may be a quick fix, or it may be something you need to work on over time. There is a problem solving worksheet in the back of this book you can use as a template.

3. *Art Journal* – In this journal you express your thoughts and feelings through drawing, painting, colouring, photography, sculpture or any other art

medium that suits you. You can do it daily, weekly or whenever you feel you need to. Art in itself has lots of therapeutic properties. You may notice a pattern to your drawing. The colours you choose may express your feelings at the time.

Expression though art is an excellent way to get to know yourself and can be a great emotional release. Concentrating on the canvas can distract you from the real world for a short time. We all need some sort of getaway and solace from time to time. Art journaling is also a great alternative to writing, if that's not your thing. You can of course combine art and writing in one journal.

4. *Gratitude Journal* – This is really good for trying to control negative feelings. Instead of dwelling on the bad, you are focusing on the good. Every day you write what you are grateful for that day and what went well. Gratitude can go a long way in lifting your mood. No matter how you feel or how bad your day has been there is always something to be grateful for no matter how small it may be.

Once you have decided which type of journaling suits you best, it's time to get started. You may even choose to combine journals which is absolutely fine. Looking at blank pages can be really daunting, but don't let it overwhelm you. Make sure you pick a journal to suit your needs. If you are going to do the art journal then make sure you pick a notebook that doesn't have any bleed through the paper.

If you are going to write in a journal daily, then pick one with quite a few pages, compared to a journal you are going to write in weekly. Now just write or draw. Easier said than done I hear you say, but don't overthink it. None of it needs to be in any order. You can date the pages if you want to. Write or draw whatever comes into your head first. If you are struggling to write a paragraph, try a mind map or a brain dump, where you just write single words or a single paragraph of whatever comes in to your mind first.

The same can be done with art. If you are struggling, then doodle for a while and you may find images flood into your head quickly and consistently. You then need to decide on a routine for journaling. You need to make it a priority if you want to use it as a therapeutic tool. Consistency is key. You can write, daily, weekly or monthly, but the most important part is that you keep it up. Set time aside in your schedule specifically for journaling. Don't worry if you are short of time, you don't need to write or draw a lot each time. A few sentences or a quick sketch will do. Something is better than nothing.

Find a quiet time away from distractions so your flow isn't interrupted. Time alone is also great for recharging, even if it is only for a short time. Most of all, just try and learn and grow from the experience. Ultimately, it should be a positive activity that helps you sort through your muddled brain, and help you find clarity.

You will start to see some life changing results within a few months, if not a few weeks of journaling. Free your emotions and start to heal from within. It will also give you a record to look back on in years to come and you will see how far you have come and you will see how much you have changed.

Which type of journaling are you most drawn to and why?

....

....

....

....

Poetry

When I was a teenager I wrote a lot of poetry. Some good, some shockingly bad. I did have a few published in anthologies and I was really proud of that. I occasionally write poetry now.

Poetry can really help you understand yourself more. Unlike journaling, you have to really think about the words and how they fit to together, creating rhythm and using alliteration. It doesn't mean your poems have to rhyme, because the majority of poems don't. Picking specific words to express your feelings can feel like you have an armour, and the words are your weapon against the enemy we call depression.

Don't expect to be a poet extraordinaire straight away, it's a skill that takes time. Your first few will probably be crap, and read like a five-year-old wrote them, and that's absolutely fine.

You can also find great emotional comfort in reading poetry. Now, if I'm being honest I was put off reading poetry in school, because I was forced to do it, but as I became an adult I saw the beauty in the words, and I connected with the sentiments and messages.

Some of my favourite poems I turn to when I'm having a tough time include:

Dylan Thomas - Do not go gentle into that good night

John Keats - Ode on Melancholy

Henry Longfellow - The rainy day

William Ernest Henley - Invictus

They are all beautiful in different ways.

• • •

What are your favourite poems? Why not read one now?

If you have never read any poetry, you are missing out, and I highly recommend you look up the ones I've listed.

....

....

....

....

If any ideas for poems have popped into your head, write them here so you don't forget:

....

....

....

....

....

....

....

....

• • •

Creative writing and story telling

Turning your negative feelings into a story is easier than you think. Take those feelings and give them to your fictional characters. Let them play those emotions out and you can decide how the story progresses and ends. Give them a happy ending. Give them the ending you want, and the one you deserve. Craft a world you can escape to. Immerse yourself in places you have always wanted to go, experience what you have always wanted feel, all through your writing.

I love crime fiction. When I was younger I wanted to be a detective. I read all the books I could find and watched all the TV shows and films. So now I sometimes write about crime and being a detective. For 30 minutes a day I pretend I'm DCI Emily Foster, and I fight crime like nobody's business. You can be anyone you want to be and travel anywhere you want to go, all through your writing.

Do you have any story ideas or character names, profiles or settings?

Write them here now:

....

....

....

....

....

....

....

....

Letter writing

Letter writing is a dying art. Writing letters doesn't mean you ever have to send them. Like I said at the start of this book, everything you write is for your eyes only, unless you decide otherwise.

Write to everyone you think has wronged you. Let loose with your feelings. Get down every negative emotion. Fold it over, stick it in an envelope and seal it. You could even burn them. Some people find this very cleansing and ritualistic. Let go of the negative feelings as the paper burns. On the other hand, you can also write to the people you want to thank and the people who have always been there for you or inspired you. If you want to send them, do so, if not that is 100% your choice.

You can write one off letters or you could make it a weekly or monthly ritual. I write to authors who have inspired me. I love snail mail.

Write a letter to your future self. Write it as though everything you want to achieve has already happened. Use the dedicated space at the back of this book or write it on a piece of paper and seal it in an envelope.

Here's a letter I wrote to myself recently. I was asked to do it by my university lecturer, and it will be opened when I graduate in 2020:

Dear Natalie,

Congratulations on graduating. You actually did it. I bet you and everyone else can't believe it. You proved yourself wrong! You came to university to change how mental health is viewed, and get a better understanding of your own depression and you have achieved this.

By now you have had your books published and been quite successful. Your goal was a minimum of three books, one per year.

I hope you now have control of your depression and are happy now. You should also be debt free now if you followed your plan.

All you ever wanted was to make your kids and family happy. You wanted to show yourself that you didn't always give up on everything. You stuck at this and you should be proud.

Mental health and social care are what you are meant to do. You are meant to help people and you are meant to do this through your writing. I hope you are confident in your abilities now. Stop doubting yourself.

You are strong and now you have worked hard to be independent. You never have to rely on ANYONE. You are making a difference in people's lives.

WELL DONE!

Emails

If you are technologically minded then this may be a better option for you.

This works along the same lines as the letters. Set up a folder in your email account and save them all there. Most of us use email every day, so it can easily be incorporated into you daily routine if you wanted.

Morning Pages

As the name suggests, this is something that is done

in the morning. As soon as you wake up to be more precise. The idea is to fill three sides of A4 paper with whatever thoughts are in your head. It doesn't have to be anything specific. Just write exactly what you are thinking. You will probably notice the first page doesn't make much sense, but as you write page two and three you may become more coherent. There is no wrong way to write morning pages.

Writing first thing will help you clear out your brain. You may find it helps you to boost productivity as you are starting with a clean slate every morning. For it to be a long term benefit you should do it for a specific time period, for example, every day for a month. Some people like to do it longer, and some people struggle to write every day for a month. To see any changes, it needs to be some sort of prolonged time period. Maybe set a goal of every morning for a week and you will probably find you want to carry on.

Blogging

Don't panic, not all blogs have to be public. If you are not confident about putting your thoughts out there, you don't have to. One day you might want to share everything and starting a blog, that can later be made public or just shared with certain people, is a great way to release your feelings.

· · ·

What can you take away from this chapter that will help you?

....

....

....

....

....

....

....

....

....

....

....

....

....

....

....

SOCIAL MEDIA ISN'T YOUR FRIEND

(OR A GOOD IDEA WHEN YOU ARE DEPRESSED)

"Someone else is happy with less than what you
have."

Author Unknown

Nine times out of ten social media will make you feel
a lot worse about yourself, especially when you are
having a particularly bad day. So, do your best to
avoid it when this is happening. It's addictive, and I
will admit that I spend way too much time on it. I
downloaded an app recently that showed me exactly
how much time I was spending on each social media
platform. I was shocked and ashamed that I wasted
that much time every day, while complaining I never

have time for anything else. It was a reality check, and gave me the kick I needed to make a change.

The first thing I did was get rid of my personal Facebook profile. I have a different one now, with no friends added, that I use to follow pages I like, and keep my business active. I'm so glad I did, and it's saving me at least an hour a day. I suggest getting an app and you will be surprised about the amount of time you waste on social media. Your mobile phone may already have this facility and an option to warn you when you are reaching a set limit of your choice. I know if you run a business then you need social media, but you can spend half an hour a day scheduling your posts, then you can forget about it and go about your day. You could even outsource your social media, if you really wanted to cut your time down.

* * *

It's really easy to look at people you follow and admire on social media and be jealous of their lives, but trust me if you look hard or even sometimes not so hard, you will always have something they don't. You might have children, be able to drive, have a degree, good skin, be talented at singing. I guarantee at least one person you follow will be wishing they had that one thing you have, the one thing that makes you special.

Nobody's life is perfect!

Social media is a distorted and filtered version of real life. People show you what they want you to see. Take my platforms for instance. I do sometimes post about bad days and I did this a lot more on Facebook. I annoyed myself with how negative I was. This was one of the main reasons I decided to get rid of it. On Twitter, I occasionally post about depression, which I mentioned at the beginning of the book. I want people to know I go through the same things they do. I retweet more on depression than I personally post. But on the whole, I try and post positive things. I don't want to damage myself or my brand and negativity breeds negativity. However, everyone has bad days and showing those is what makes us human.

Social media doesn't need to be a bad thing in your life. I follow other authors and it spurs me on. I enjoy watching beauty vloggers on YouTube. Watching these videos gives me an escape. I highly recommend following people you admire because they will help you strive for better. Just remember they are real people with real problems just like you and me, even if they don't show them.

I follow some really motivational people on my social media. Some are more well-known than others. I watch a lot of writing videos and these helped me to finish this book. Through social media I participated in a challenge to write 50,000 words in a month. Writers' supporting writers' is always an amazing thing. I also found beta readers for this book through social media, so you can see, sometimes social media can be a great thing.

We all have to remember, no matter how we feel, there is always someone worse off than us. We all need a reminder sometimes and it can be easy to fall into the 'woe is me' mindset. Depression does that to you. It plays with your mind and makes you believe things are so bad that there is no way out. There is! Depression is not worth dying for! I will probably repeat this several times in the book.

So, right now you are probably thinking, well she can't be depressed or she doesn't know how it really feels. Trust me I do, and I have had suicidal thoughts in the past. I have sat there thinking everyone would be better off without me and that the only way the pain would go away was if I was dead. It's just not true. This statement alone shows that depression made me selfish.

Of course, my life matters. I have people who love me. You do too, no matter what depression tells you. Depression is a liar. It lies, cheats, manipulates and controls you. It's like being in an emotionally abusive relationship. But you can get out of it! You never have to stay in a situation like that.

You can be strong. YOU ARE STRONG. Repeat this to yourself.

Choose who you follow on social media wisely. Pick people who are going after their dreams. Pick people who have fought mental health issues and have come out the other side, they give the best advice because they truly know what it feels like. Doctors, Psychologists and Cognitive Behavioural Therapists are great and a must, but they cannot truly understand how you feel if they haven't experienced it themselves. I talk about this more in the 'Professional help' chapter. They say it takes a village to raise a child, well it takes an army to fight depression. No person knows everything or has all the answers. Use the resources available, that's what they are there for. Why else would these jobs exist if millions and millions of other people before you and after you didn't need them too?

Which social media platforms do you use? (List them here)

....

....

....

....

....

....

Which is your favourite and why?

....

....

....

....

....

Which is your least favourite and why?

....

....

....

....

....

• • •

Do you think you can stop using your least favourite platform? If no why not?

....

....

....

....

....

....

....

....

Have you just made an excuse that's not valid for why you can't get rid of one platform? STOP MAKING EXCUSES. You survived before social media and you will after it. You DO NOT need every platform not matter what you tell yourself. You may be addicted to social media if the thought of getting rid of a platform, even the one you use the least worries you.

As I explained earlier I got rid of my personal Facebook page and it's helped me a lot. I don't see other people's drama, I'm not sucked into thinking my friends lives are better than mine and feelings of jealousy are much less now.

Try cutting down how much time you spend on one of the platforms and unfollow/unfriend those who are not truly friends. Don't be worried about offending anyone. They will get over it. Your mental health is more important.

Gradually over time start doing the same on all platforms. I now only follow people I admire and fellow writers on Twitter. I have no friends on Facebook, I just follow pages of people who inspire me and the same goes for the other platforms. It doesn't stop all my negative comparison thoughts, but truthfully it has made a huge difference. Comparing ourselves to others is human nature. It's how we react to the comparison that matters. There will always be someone doing better and always someone doing worse than you.

Take the apps off your phone and only access them via a laptop or desktop computer. This will also drastically cut down on the time you waste online. Do it one app per month or even per week if you think you can do this.

Which app could you take off your phone right now?

....

....

....

....

....

....

....

....

Download or use the tracker app on your phone as mentioned before, and for seven days write here how much time you spent on social media:

....

....

....

....

....

....

....

• • •

Rise of the internet troll

I'm sure we have experienced an internet troll at some point whether it be our own little monster or someone else's. There are people who spend their day plotting to ruin others. Sad, I know, but that says a lot about them, and nothing about you. (See the third quote in the 'My story' chapter). If they were truly happy then they would have better things to do. We have all looked at someone and thought, I hate you, I'm jealous of you, you've put weight on, but most of us have the self-control to keep it to ourselves.

Internet trolls don't. They want to see other people unhappy because they are unhappy. I don't care if you are depressed, there is no excuse for being horrible and trying to bring someone else down. If you ever go to leave a nasty comment on social media, stop and think about why you are doing it? Will it make you feel better? Why do you think it is okay to be nasty to someone else?

How did the internet troll make you feel?

....

....

....

....

....

....

....

....

How did you deal with the situation / person?

....

....

....

....

....

....

....

....

What would you do differently next time?

....

....

....

....

....

....

....

....

When you are depressed anything someone says to you that's negative or given as constructive criticism, you are going to take to heart. When I was particularly low, I tweeted a message with a typo and someone pointed it out. It made me literally question if I ever wanted to write again. Something so silly that happens to everyone at some point (because autocorrect hates us all) got so blown out of proportion in my mind. Depression does that. She takes silly little things and turns them into major issues.

The best way to deal with trolls, that I have found is to delete and block. Don't engage. Don't stoop to their level and never give them the attention they crave. Don't feed the monster. Don't worry about looking too sensitive if you delete comments. This is your social media space, you can do what you want with it.

You can't change someone's opinion by arguing with them. Sometimes you have to agree to disagree, and be comfortable with your own choices. Arguing only upsets you and the other person. Tit for tat is pointless.

Just keep it positive.

What can you take away from this chapter that will help you?

....

....

....

....

....

....

....

....

....

....

....

....

6

CHANGING DESTRUCTIVE HABITS

"The quickest path to self-destruction is to push away the people you love."

Cassia Leo, Pieces of You

People who've never had depression can't fully understand what it's like. Some are more understanding and patient than others. They have sympathy and in some cases, can empathise, and they will stick by you no matter what. Then there are those who are closed minded and see things in black and white.

I'm sure you have heard most of the following statements:

- *Just snap out of it!*
- *Why are you always so miserable?*
- *Just get over yourself!*
- *Why are you so anti-social?*
- *What is wrong with you?*
- *You have a great life, what have you got to be depressed about?*

For someone who's never been in the depths of despair, it's hard to understand depression. It's not their fault. Depression is a taboo subject, so there isn't as much information out there for people to take in and understand. The word depression is also thrown around alot. 'I spilled my drink on my white dress, I'm so depressed', or 'The TV show I love has finished, it's so depressing.' None of these statements are true depression. They are a temporary sadness, and not to be confused with chronic clinical depression.

People are getting better at talking about it, but there is still a long way to go. There's a stigma attached to depression. When you hear people say things to you like 'cheer up, it's not that bad', it's easy to get angry or withdraw even more. Anger builds up and then more self-destructive behaviour occurs. We need to stop letting people control our emotions. I'm a fine one to talk and I'm still working on this, so it would be good if we could do this together.

Next time someone says something insensitive don't bottle it up. Come back to this book and write down what they said and how it made you feel:

....

....

....

....

....

....

....

....

....

....

....

....

....

. . .

People say a lot of stupid shit. Never apologise for being you and never change for someone else.

"Be who you are and say what you feel, because those who mind don't matter, and those who matter don't mind."

Bernard M Baruch

We have around 60,000 thoughts a day, and the majority of them if you are depressed, are negative. You are reading this book for a reason and it's probably not because you are feeling good and having amazingly positive thoughts. That's what we need to change. We are going to tip the balance from negative to positive. It's easy to form bad habits and continue with harmful self-talk. We need to recognise our triggers and stop them before they escalate. You are not stupid or worthless. You are enough, and you are here for a reason!

From now on we will be forming positive, life changing habits. It's said to take 21 days to form a habit and 90 days for it to become a permanent change in your life. For the next 21 days, you are going to write down something you did well, every day. There is a worksheet at the back of the book for this. After 21 days, you should be in the habit of positive self-talk and hopefully it will continue.

For your 90 day challenge I want you to do something every day than makes you feel good. This runs alongside the 21-day challenge but obviously continues for 90 days. Once the 90 days are over it will be embedded into your way of life.

Here are some examples of what makes me feel good, so you get the idea.

- Painting my nails
- Reading
- Colouring
- Watching a TV show
- Writing
- Going for a walk
- Taking a bubble bath
- Listening to music

Highlight the behaviours that apply to you:

Self-sabotage

Repeating mistakes

Forced incompetence

Self-harm

Self-pity

Sabotaging relationships

Mental neglect

Physical neglect

Hiding emotions

Social suicide

Refusing help

Failure to take action

Overeating

Undereating

Binge drinking

Drug taking

Antisocial behaviour

Unnecessary self-sacrifice

Violence

Verbally abusive

Threatening suicide

Common destructive behaviours

Drugs and alcohol

Depression can lead to substance abuse and substance abuse can lead to depression. Drugs and alcohol can alter the brains chemistry. Substance abuse is common for those with depression and other mental illnesses.

Mostly substances are abused to self-medicate and numb mental pain. Drugs and alcohol can block symptoms and many use them as a coping mechanism. But the problems are still there when the high or hangover goes. Drugs and alcohol can negatively impact all aspects of your life and are not the answer for coping with depression.

Have you noticed you have been drinking more alcohol recently?

....

....

....

....

If yes, how much are you drinking per day or week?

....

....

....

....

....

Are you taking illegal drugs or abusing prescription ones?

....

....

....

....

....

....

....

. . .

If yes, what are you taking and how often?

....

....

....

....

....

....

....

....

If you have said yes to either of those questions, you need to seek help straight away. Talk to someone you trust or make an appointment to see your doctor.

Eating

Depression can change your eating habits.

Some people may turn to food for comfort, overeat and put on an unhealthy amount of weight. Others might purposely under eat or they lose their appetite and unintentionally shed too much weight. Skipping meals is common as depression can suppress your appetite. In either case it can also be a form of control. When everything seems to be going wrong, food may seem like the only thing you are able to control.

If you notice you are overeating or under eating or purposely using food as the only thing you think you can control, you need to ask for help now.

Have you noticed a change in your eating habits? If so, how?

....

....

....

....

....

....

Are you using food as a form of control?

....

....

....

··
··
··
··
··

Sleep

Poor quality sleep will have a huge impact on your depression. It can be a catch 22 situation where a lack of quality sleep can cause depression, or you are unable to sleep or sleep too much because of depression. You may become irritable, stressed, anxious, unable to function properly in the day, lethargic and generally unwell.

You may have noticed you are sleeping a lot more. Hypersomnia is the opposite of insomnia where you feel like you need to sleep a lot and do so, but are still tired no matter how many hours you are getting. Insomnia is when you find it difficult to fall asleep or when you do, you can't stay asleep for long.

In the self-care chapter of this book I've listed some

ways to get a better night's sleep, so give them a try if you are struggling. If they don't work then see your doctor.

How well do you sleep?

....

....

....

....

....

....

....

....

On average how many hours a night do you sleep undisturbed?

....

....

....

....

•   •   •

Unhealthy relationships

Look at the people you surround yourself with. Are they contributing to your destructive behaviour? If the answer is yes, then you need to remove them from your life. Change is difficult when you are constantly surrounded by negative influences. You need to have a circle of friends and family that support you and want you to do better.

Toxic relationships can be with parents, other family members, friends, partners and even co-workers. If anyone in your life leaves you feeling drained, bad about yourself, in danger, taken advantage of, like you need to change to please them or are constantly bringing drama into your life then these are signs you have an unhealthy relationship.

Co-dependency is another form. If you can't function properly without another person, then this is very unhealthy. A counsellor can help you with this and give you the tools you need to gain back your independence.

Are you in an unhealthy or co-dependent relationship? If yes, who with?

....

....

....

....

....

....

....

....

Anger

Depression can often manifest as anger. Up until a few years ago my depression displayed itself as sadness, irritability and lethargy. While these still remain, three years ago I also began to become very angry. If something bothered me my temper was quick and I would scream and shout. It's much better now and I attribute that to the people I surround myself with. Three years ago, I had relationships with people who were very volatile, but I removed them from my life in 2018. I still feel anger building up now on occasion, and I will admit I take it out on the people closest to me. I feel like shit after, especially if I've screamed at the kids for something silly, but it's much more controlled now and I can manage it better.

Most anger stems from frustration and not being able to control a situation. Help is available to manage your anger and find more suitable ways to express your emotions.

Do you think you have an anger issue?

....

....

....

....

....

If yes, what do you think triggers your anger?

....

....

....

....

....

....

. . .

What will you do to take control of it?

....

....

....

....

....

....

....

Spending

It's easy to focus on what we don't have rather than what we do have. We take for granted what we have and think it's always going to be there. That's just not true. We are never satisfied with what we have and always want more. There lies the problem and the route to unhappiness. We don't need anything to survive except food, water and shelter and some argue love, which I believe wholeheartedly. So why do we feel like we need all the up to date technology, the fanciest clothes and the biggest houses? Material things, no matter what anyone says will never bring true happiness because it's all superficial.

Love of 'things' is not real. It's love for people we need. Kindness, compassion and love are all free, and will make you a million times happier than a new car or a designer bag.

Material things give instant gratification and that's why we are drawn to them. When I'm very depressed I spend a lot. Usually I buy books or clothes. I look forward to them arriving, and for a few hours I'm happy, then the hole appears again and I want more gratification. Of course, I'm never going to be fulfilled this way, and when I'm having a better day I can see this, and get angry with myself for buying such silly things. I have recently found that it may not be the act of buying 'stuff' that gives me the gratification. When I get a book from the library, or win anything, I get the same feeling. I think it's the excitement of having something I've never had before.

Our brains look for something that will make us happy quickly, when we are depressed. But true fulfilment and happiness can only come from loving yourself first. Things don't love you, people do, but if you don't love yourself, or at least like yourself, how can you expect anyone else to? This statement isn't a revelation.

• • •

What do you do or spend money on for instant gratification?

....

....

....

....

....

....

....

....

Has that ever made you happy?

....

....

....

....

....

....

....

. . .

Sex, self-harm, reckless driving and gambling are some other forms of destructive behaviours, as well as many, many more. If you recognise your behaviour as destructive, then as I keep saying, and will continue to say, ASK FOR HELP!

Changing your behaviour

To be able to change your behaviour you need to acknowledge what behaviours are harmful, and admit why you are doing certain harmful activities. You can't turn off your emotions but you can take control of them and change the way you react to certain situations.

Which of the common destructive behaviours are happening in your life right now? It's not uncommon for there to be multiple behaviours.

....

....

....

....

....

....

....

....

Pick one destructive behaviour at a time to change. More than one may overwhelm, and state why you chose this one first:

....

....

....

....

....

....

....

....

Identify why you have been on this destructive path. For example, you've been drinking to relax or taking drugs to conform due to peer pressure. What is the trigger or reason?

• • •

Relax

Reduce stress

Have fun

Conforming

Insecure

Provide short-term relief

Anger

Avoidance

Numbing

Attention

Control

Revenge

Write any here that are not listed:

....

....

....

....

....

• • •

What have been the consequences of your destructive behaviours so far?

Blackouts

Hangovers

Poor decisions

Hurting others

Poor health

Illegal activity

Lost relationships

Debt

Unemployment

Write any here that are not listed:

....

....

....

....

....

....

• • •

Why do you want to change your behaviour?

....

....

....

....

....

....

....

....

What needs to happen for a change to occur? What action will you take? (e.g. counsellor, AA)

....

....

....

....

....

....

• • •

When, where and how will you take action?

....

....

....

....

....

....

....

....

How will you ensure you keep up positive action?

....

....

....

....

....

....

....

....

• • •

Get support from someone you trust. Who will this be?

....

....

....

....

....

....

"Incredible change happens in your life when you decide to take control of what you do have power over instead of craving control over what you don't."

Steve Maraboli

What can you take away from this chapter that will help you?

....

....

....

....

....

7

SELF-CARE

"Things do not grow better; they remain as they are. It is we who grow better, by changes we make in ourselves."

Swami Vivekananda

In this chapter I want to cover what you can do to help yourself, that doesn't include medication or other people. No matter what you do, if you are prescribed medication, take it! Never stop unless you have discussed it with a doctor first.

When you start to feel better it can be easy to think you don't need the medication. You definitely do, for now anyway, because it's the medication that's making you feel better. Don't fall into the trap of thinking you are feeling good, so you don't need it anymore. Never forget, depression is a sneaky bitch and will make you think things that aren't totally true; yet. Just because you are taking medication, it doesn't mean you shouldn't try self-care methods. Attack this bitch from all directions!

It's time to put yourself first. You can't look after other people if you don't look after yourself. Running around after everyone else may make you feel needed, but truly the most important person who needs you, is YOU. Yes, that includes if you have kids, look after a sick relative or any other situation like that. Stop trying to make everyone else happy before yourself and, STOP SAYING YES TO SHIT YOU HATE!

I think this quote sums it up:

"I think the saddest people always try their hardest to make people happy because they know what it's like to feel absolutely worthless and they don't want anyone else to feel like that."

Robin Williams

This is very noble, but imagine how happy you could make them if you were happy first. Make yourself a priority.

There are lots of ways to care for yourself.

Music

Have you ever noticed how your mood can change when you listen to music.? A breakup song will make you feel sad and a dance track can energise you. Sometimes it can feel like the lyrics of a song are specifically written for you.

Music is powerful.

I have a playlist on my phone full of songs specifically for when I'm having a bad day. They are uplifting songs with a powerful message. The folder is called 'Get fucking going', but obviously you can name yours whatever you like. The songs usually have a fast beat and I can turn them up really loud and soak in the vibes. The type to get your heart racing.

What type of music do you listen to and why?

....

....

....

....

....

....

....

....

Which songs make you feel good? Put them all in a playlist now.

....

....

....

....

....

....

....

Reading/Bibliotherapy

Reading is the best escape there is. Forget your problems and lose yourself in the pages of another world.

When reading fiction, try and choose feel good books. There is no point reading something dark, it won't help your thoughts.

I read a lot of self-help books. They have definitely had a positive impact on my life and attitudes. I've listed some of the ones I found most helpful for my mindset in the back of this book.

Changing the quality of your thinking is really important. Books can help you do that. They expand your horizons and show you things are not black and white. The world is beautiful and there for the taking.

When you are depressed, reading may sound like the last thing you want to do, because honesty just getting out of bed is a massive task and achievement in itself. I've had times when I've had to force myself to read, but I've always been glad I did. Once you start reading, if the book is good enough it will only take a few sentences to keep you wanting more. If you are short on time then try audiobooks. You can listen to them while doing chores or driving to work.

If you can't afford books or magazines, then pop to your local library. There are also lots of magazines you can read online and you can join websites such as BookBub as a reader. I get daily emails from them and they have books discounted and free.

Many libraries also offer eBooks you can download directly to your device, so check if your local library offer this service.

What types of books do you like to read and why?

....

....

....

....

....

....

....

....

Adult Colouring

I was so happy to see this trend come back a few years ago. At the time of writing this, it has died down, but I still enjoy it. I use colouring to relax and unwind. It can have calming effects and there's something really peaceful about sitting with a pencil or felt tip pen and concentrating on making something look beautiful. I'm rubbish at art, but colouring makes me feel accomplished. It's not just for kids.

Have you tried adult colouring? If you have what do you like to colour the most? I love mandalas.

....

....

....

....

....

....

....

....

Art

I'm terrible at drawing. Even my handwriting is shocking. I got told off a lot in school about it and had to use special adaptors on pencils. Needless to say, they didn't work. Thank God for word processors.

Even though I am rubbish it still doesn't stop me trying. Painting on canvas is my favourite. I don't do shapes I usually do blocks of colour. I don't show anyone and you don't have to either. I enjoy painting with my kids. Although they are better than me, so it can be a bit annoying. One person's trash is another one's treasure, remember that. You can also get some great paint by numbers on canvas that have great results.

What type of art do you like to create?

....

....

....

....

....

....

....

....

If you don't create any, what type of art interests you the most?

....

....

....

....

• • •

Knitting, sewing, crochet and other crafts

According to some recent university studies published. crochet and knitting improves mental health. Crafts such as pottery, scrapbooking, knitting, sewing, crochet and cross-stitch can be used to ease stress. Working with your hands can have a positive impact on your mental health. Creating can give a sense of achievement and fulfilment. It's also great for focus and teaches patience as well as problem solving skills. Crafting has also been reported to be really helpful in fighting the onset of dementia and PTSD.

Do you already craft?

....

....

....

....

....

If yes, which do you enjoy?

....

....

....

....

If no, which would you like to try?

....

....

....

....

If you already craft is there another type you would like to try?

....

....

....

....

....

I knit and crochet. I would like to try sewing and have been looking at purchasing a sewing machine.

• • •

Meditation

Do you practice meditation? I used to think it was all a bit hippy dippy, but that's because I hadn't tried it. Now, I'm not one that 'ums and ahs'. I just like to sit quietly, on my own and try to clear my mind. Sometimes it's easier said than done with three kids, but at least I try, right?

In this day and age (wow I sound old) we never switch off. Mobile phones by our beds, Wi-Fi constantly on. How can we expect our brains to switch off when we never switch off the technology? We have to make a conscious effort to unplug, literally and metaphorically. It doesn't have to be for a long time. We can't all find hours of spare time to meditate, but I'm sure if we put down our phones and turned the TV off we could find ten minutes.

Try unplugging for ten minutes today and just sit quietly. Then write how you felt after here:

....

....

....

....

....

....

. . .

Complementary therapies

As I said at the beginning of the book, I'm not a doctor, so before trying any complementary therapies, consult yours. They are not suitable for everyone, such as pregnant women and those with certain health issues. Always air on the side of caution and seek advice first.

Some you might like to consider if you are given the okay are:

Acupuncture - Fine needles are inserted into identified parts of the skin corresponding to certain organs of the body. Acupuncture is said to unblock congestion. It's also known for releasing endorphins and stimulating the body's natural pain killers.

Aromatherapy - The use of essential oils can be used to alleviate depression symptoms. Aromatherapy is thought to reduce anxiety levels, boost the immune system, help with sleep issues, headaches and more.

Different oils are used and mixed for certain uses. They can be used for massage or diffused into the air. Research and advice should be sought before trying any essential oils.

Massage therapy - It won't cure your depression but it might go a long way in relieving tension and help you to relax. Massage is good for fatigue and sleeping problems.

There are different types of massage including, Swedish, deep tissue, Shiatsu, reflexology and hot stone. You will need to choose depending on your need.

Hypnotherapy - This can be used in conjunction with other treatments for depression. It works by putting you in a trance and accessing your subconscious. It is thought that you are more susceptible to suggestion when under hypnosis. It can then be used to replace trauma with positive thoughts and feelings and eliminate self-sabotaging thoughts.

WITH ALL OF THE ABOVE OPTIONS ONLY EVER GO TO A TRAINED PROFESSIONAL AND CHECK THEIR REVIEWS AND RECOMMENDATIONS BEFORE ANY TREATMENT TAKES PLACE.

Exercise

I hate exercise, but it's a necessity. You need a healthy body to have a healthy mind. I've tried the gym and jogging and it's not for me, so I do yoga at home and skipping. I watch YouTube videos or put on a yoga DVD that was bought for me many Christmases ago when I decided exercise was my 'new thing'. I don't drive yet, so I walk a lot. I used to hate the thought of walking anywhere, but now I prefer it over public transport. I hate the thought of exercise and I really have to talk myself into it every time, but I feel great after. It wakes me up and gives me the energy I need. It reminds me I'm alive when I can feel my heart racing. Otherwise I'm rotting away on the sofa or in bed.

What's your favourite type of exercise?

....

....

....

....

....

....

How do you feel after exercising?

....

....

....

....

• • •

If you don't exercise yet, which type interests you the most and why?

....

....

....

....

....

....

....

....

Food and drink

I used to hate cooking. Anything I could do to avoid it I would. I chose takeaways and simple meals like beans on toast, over preparing anything nutritious. As I've gotten older and more aware of what my kids eat, I experiment more and now I actually don't mind cooking, and I'm not that bad at it. I try to eat healthily but being honest I eat chocolate and drink fizzy pop. I don't want to deprive myself and end up feeling worse. It's all about moderation.

Cooking can be enjoyable and a hobby that can be used as a distraction technique. Distraction will only work for a while though. You will eventually have to deal with depression head on if you want to get better.

There are some foods that can help with your mood or worsen it.

Food & drink that can positively affect your mood:

Oily fish

Tomato

Nuts

Mushrooms

Olive oils

Bananas

Milk

Apples

Cheese

Green leafy salad

Eggs

Potatoes

•   •   •

Drinking water is extremely important. I can hear you saying you hate water. Trust me, I do too, but there are some serious health benefits to consuming water. Water is great for your concentration and lowering stress levels. Not drinking enough can cause dehydration, headaches, nausea and confusion. You should be drinking half of your body weight in ounces of water. So, if you weigh 120 pounds you should be drinking 60 ounces of water a day. Yes, it's a lot and yes you will become friendly with the bathroom. But it's what your body needs to function to the best of its ability.

Foods/drinks that can negatively affect your mood

Anything with a high sugar content and alcohol.

Eating and drinking too many simple sugars could influence your depression. Sugar is addictive. The high from it can be more pleasurable than drugs like cocaine. It's also readily available and cheap. It's in everything from soups to croissants. In many instances the sugar is hidden, so it's important to know what to look out for on labels.

The addiction to sugar can be broken by slowly cutting it out of your diet. It might take some time if you have only really eaten processed foods. Replace the sugar with whole foods such as fruit, vegetables, grains and lean meats.

Do you eat a lot of processed and junk foods? List ones you eat.

....

....

....

....

....

....

....

....

What healthy foods do you eat?

....

....

....

....

....

. . .

If you could make a meal from scratch, right now, what would it be?

....

....

....

Why not make it then? There's nothing stopping you. If it's the first time making it and it goes wrong, so what? Try again. If it goes right then imagine how you are going to feel. Just do it!

Sleep

Sleep isn't just about rest. It's important for recovery and energy. Sleep can be greatly affected when you are depressed. You may not be able to sleep or you may be sleeping too much. Lack of sleep can make it hard for you to manage your feelings and think clearly. These things are already difficult when you are depressed.

Creating a routine and sticking to it can be helpful in creating good sleep patterns. Throughout the day there are things you can do to aid a good night's sleep. These include:

- Exercise. Even a short gentle walk will help.
- Get fresh air. Kill two birds with one stone and exercise outside. Daylight is good for your body's natural sleep-wake cycle.
- Eat regular meals. Try and eat at the same time every day. Don't eat too close to bedtime. Also limit alcohol and caffeine as these will keep you awake.
- Switch off all devices at least an hour before bed. Switching off devices gives your brain a chance to switch off.
- Meditate before bed to become calm and relaxed. Let go of any negativity from the day.
- Make the bedroom as dark as possible.
- Keep the bedroom for sex and sleeping only. No TV!
- Take a warm bath before you get in to bed.

What can you incorporate into your routine today?

....

....

....

....

• • •

Ecotherapy

Ecotherapy is about outdoor activities and connecting with nature. Activities range from conservation and farming, to walks, cycling, animal care and woodland exploration.

It helps with depression by, facilitating outdoor exercise, creating social interactions if done in group settings, and being surrounded by nature can naturally boost your mood. It's also great for mindfulness. It helps you become attuned to your natural surroundings and be present in the moment.

Which form of ecotherapy interests you the most and why?

....

....

....

....

....

....

....

• • •

Cleaning

For some, cleaning will be the last thing you want to do. Lack of motivation is not uncommon and can cause chores to pile up. It can get to a point where it's hard to know where to start, so you don't. It becomes a cycle of feeling bad for not cleaning, but feeling too low to motivate yourself.

The key is to do little and often. Start with something small like putting a load in the washing machine then have a break. Then move on to putting dishes away. Making a list of a few tasks to do per day and then ticking them off may be motivating for you. Cleaning a room per day may be a good start.

Write here what you are going to do first.

....

....

What can you take away from this chapter that will help you?

....

....

....

....

....

....

....

....

....

....

....

....

....

....

....

....

....

....

....

8

PROFESSIONAL HELP

"The strong individual is the one who asks for help
when he needs it."

Rona Barrett

Whether you believe in professional help or not it
will never hurt to accept advice. Many people are put
off seeking professional help for depression because
it has a stigma attached to it, which I went over earlier in the book. But think of it this way, if you have a
headache you take a paracetamol, if you break your
arm it's set in a cast, and if you have an infection you
take antibiotics. How is taking a tablet to help your
depression any different? Just because it's your mind

it doesn't mean it's any less important or should be seen as something weak. I'm proud I asked for help because without it I don't know if I would be here to tell you this now.

When you go to see your doctor, they will more than likely recommend a counsellor. Say yes! Talking to a stranger is more therapeutic than you know. People say it's sometimes easier to open up to a stranger and I believe this. Also, the professional is never going to judge you and they can give you tools you will probably never have thought of before. You don't have to be referred by a doctor, you can make an appointment yourself.

There are three main types of help available. These aren't the only services to access, but they are the most common and may vary in different countries:

Counselling

I've already said it, but talking helps and heals. Counselling is an opportunity to talk to someone who's neutral and none-judgmental. A counsellor's job is to listen, support and never criticise. It's all confidential and offloading to someone who doesn't know you and is impartial can help more than you know.

. . .

If you live in the UK, then you can get counselling free through the NHS. To access this, you need to speak to your General Practitioner (GP). You may have to wait a while and probably won't get a choice who you see. However, you don't need an NHS referral, you can refer yourself for psychological services.

There are many ways to undertake counselling:

- Face-to-face
- Group
- By phone
- My email
- Online (Skype, FaceTime and other video calling platforms)

It's down to what you feel most comfortable with. I hate talking on the phone, so face-to-face or email are the best options for me.

Cognitive Behavioural Therapy (CBT)

CBT is a form of counselling/therapy. A trained counsellor will listen and help you find answers to your own questions. It is used for a variety of mental health issues. It is based around the idea of how we think about things controls our subsequent behaviour. It challenges patterns and cycles of thinking. Discussions are had around how past experiences, thoughts, feelings, attitudes and current situations may be impacting the way you currently see the world. You will learn coping skills for different problems and it will give you tools to help with feelings of anxiousness, depression and sleep problems.

Psychologists/Psychotherapy

A psychologist's job involves assessment and intervention. They are highly trained mental health professionals, who help people recover from depression and other mental health illnesses.

Psychotherapy can be an effective treatment alone or combined with medication. It will help you pinpoint certain life events that may have contributed to your depression, and it will equip you with tools to accept what happened and change the way you react to situations that may arise in the future. It challenges unhelpful behaviours, develops coping skills and identifies your triggers. It will also help you set realistic goals for recovery and the future.

Psychiatrists

Most people will not need to see a psychiatrist. Help from GP's, counsellors or psychologists are usually very effective. If you do need more specialist help then you might be referred to a psychiatrist or the community mental health team if you are in the UK.

A psychiatrist is a medical doctor who treats emotional and mental disorders. They are usually likely to prescribe medication in conjunction with other treatments such as psychotherapy. Sometimes hospitalisation is required. That can sound scary, but it's for your own good and may be what's best for you at that specific time.

Write here which treatment you think would suit you best, or the one you will look into and why?

....

....

....

....

....

....

....

. . .

Details of websites, telephone numbers and email addresses you find that you could seek help and advice from:

....

....

....

....

....

....

....

....

What can you take away from this chapter that will help you?

....

....

....

....

....

9

WORKSHEETS & TRACKERS

"You must go into the dark in order to bring forth your light."

Debbie Ford, The Dark Side of the Light Chasers

The following pages are for you to keep track of your life and things that may be affecting your depression. There is enough space for two weeks of tracking. After that you can download additional pages at www.natalieroberts.net/worksheetsandtrackers, or you can use your own notebook. There are also some blank pages for any notes you might want to make at the back of this book.

· · ·

I would love to know if they worked for you and if you saw a pattern once you have filled in the sheets. You can email me at writethroughdepression@gmail.com

If you think there are any worksheets or trackers I should include in the next edition, please let me know.

GRATITUDE WORKSHEET

Every day for two weeks, write five things you are grateful for each day. Refer back to the chapter on 'Start writing now' if you need prompts.

* * *

Week 1

* * *

Monday

1..

2..

3..

4..

5..

Tuesday

1..

2..

3..

4..

5..

Wednesday

1..

2..

3..

4..

5..

Thursday

1..

2..

3...

4...

5...

Friday

1...

2...

3...

4...

5...

Saturday

1...

2...

3...

4...

5...

Sunday

1...

Gratitude worksheet

2..

3..

4..

5..

Week 2

Monday

1..

2..

3..

4..

5..

Tuesday

1..

2..

3..

4..

5..

Wednesday

1..

2..

3..

4..

5..

Thursday

1..

2..

3..

4..

5..

Friday

1..

2..

3..

4..

5..

Saturday

1..

2..

3..

4..

5..

Sunday

1..

2..

3..

4..

5..

PROBLEM SOLVING WORKSHEET

Identify the problem (who/what?)

....

....

....

What made the problem arise? (why/when?)

....

....

....

Identify 3 different ways you could resolve the problem (how?)

Problem solving worksheet

1..

2..

3..

Which resolution will you try first and why?

....

....

....

Did it work?

....

If yes, evaluate why did it work?

....

....

....

....

If no, why didn't it work and which resolution will you try next?

....

....

LETTER TO YOUR FUTURE SELF

....

....

....

....

....

....

....

....

....

....

Letter to your future self

....

....

....

....

....

....

....

....

....

....

....

....

....

....

....

LETTER TO YOUR DEPRESSION

....

....

....

....

....

....

....

....

....

....

....

Letter to your depression

....

....

....

....

....

....

....

....

....

....

....

....

....

....

....

....

DOODLE PAGE

This page is for when you have feelings you want to express artistically. Again, like writing, you don't have to be good at drawing.

If you don't know where to start, try a flower, a house or a star. These are my go-to doodles.

21 DAY CHALLENGE

For the next 21 days write one thing that you did well each day:

1...

2...

3...

4...

5...

6...

7...

8...

9...

21 day challenge

10..

11..

12..

13..

14..

15..

16..

17..

18..

19..

20..

21..

90 DAY CHALLENGE

For the next 90 days write down one thing that made
you feel good each day:

1...

2...

3...

4...

5...

6...

7...

8...

9..

10..

11..

12..

13..

14..

15..

16..

17..

18..

19..

20..

21..

22..

23..

24..

25..

27..

28..

29...

30...

31...

32...

33...

34...

35...

36...

37...

38...

39...

40...

41...

42...

43...

44...

45...

46...

47...

48...

49...

50...

51...

52...

53...

54...

55...

56...

57...

58...

59...

60...

61...

62...

63...

64...

65...

66...

67...

68...

69...

70...

71...

72...

73...

74...

75...

76...

77...

78...

79...

80...

81...

82...

83...

84...

85...

90 day challenge

86..

87..

88..

89..

90..

NOTES

....
....
....
....
....
....
....
....
....
....

Notes

....

....

....

....

....

....

....

....

....

....

....

....

....

....

....

....

....

....

....

....

....

....

....

....

....

....

....

....

....

....

....

....

....

Notes

....

....

....

....

....

....

....

....

....

....

....

....

....

....

....

....

....

SPECIAL REQUEST

I intend on doing a second edition of this book to include any new coping strategies I find helpful over the coming months and years. I would love to hear your thoughts and advice on dealing with depression so I can make the book as useful to as many people as possible.

If you enjoyed the book please recommend it to your friends and family and leave a review on Amazon, it will give me my writer wings and is also something nice to show my mum and kids.

You can submit feedback, advice and tips to writethroughdepression@gmail.com

NEWSLETTER SIGNUP

To keep up-to-date with the latest news, upcoming releases and giveaways sign up to my newsletter. I promise I will only email you once a month, unless I have any special offers and giveaways going on.

www.natalieroberts.net

RESOURCES

Books

Girl, Wash Your Face - *Rachel Hollis*

Opening up by Writing it Down - *James W. Pennebaker, PhD & Joshua M. Smythe, PhD.*

Reasons to Stay Alive - *Matt Haig*

The Shock of the Fall - *Nathan Filer*

Something Changed - *Matthew Williams*

Growing from Depression - *Dr Neel Burton*

Black Rainbows - *Rachel Kelly*

Sunbathing in the Rain - *Gwyneth Lewis*

Shoot the Damn Dog - *Sally Brampton*

Sane New World: Taming the Mind - *Ruby Wax*

Big Magic - *Elizabeth Gilbert*

The Secret, The Magic and The Power - *Rhonda Byrne*

The Compound Effect - *Darren Hardy*

Rising Strong - *Brene Brown*

Light is the New Black - *Rebecca Campbell*

The Courage to be Creative - *Doreen Virtue*

Stop Saying You're Fine - *Mel Robbins*

Podcasts

The Mind Podcast

Mentally Yours

Happy Place

Bryony Gordon's Mad World

All in the Mind

MQ Open Mind

YouTube Channels

Mind, the mental health charity

Time to Change

Rethink Mental Illness

Websites

www.relate.org.uk - Counselling service for relation-ships UK

www.mind.org.uk - Mental health charity in the UK

www.sane.org.uk - Mental health charity UK

www.depressionalliance.org - National mental health charity

www.depressionuk.org - Depression charity UK

www.rethink.org - Help people through a mental health crisis

www.anxietyuk.org.uk - National anxiety charity

www.blurtitout.org - Organisation dedicated to raising awareness of mental health issues

www.samaritans.org - 24 hour service for anyone in need/crisis

www.nhs.uk. -Expert advice and guidance

www.mentalhealth.org.uk - Dedicated to finding & addressing the sources of mental health problems

US

www.nami.org - Non-profit mental health charity US

AUS

www.sane.org - Mental health charity AUS

https://www.beyondblue.org.au - Anxiety & depression support

Important dates

World Mental Health Day - 10th October

Suicide Prevention Week - September

Mental Health Awareness Week - May

Debt Help

Stepchange.org

CapUK.org

Nationaldebthelpline.org

Turn2us.org.uk

Citizensadvice.org

US

USA.gov/debt

AUS

Ndh.org.au

ABOUT THE AUTHOR

Natalie is a freelance writer and author of self-help, personal development and social care books. She is a mental health advocate and is studying for a BSc in mental health and wellbeing.

Connect with Natalie online:

www.natalieroberts.net

facebook.com/natalierobertswriter

twitter.com/natalieroberts1

instagram.com/natalierobertwriter

GRATITUDE

This book is dedicated to anyone who has ever talked publicly about their depression. It has helped me more than you know, and made me realise I'm not a freak and that mental illness is nothing to be ashamed of.

Thanks to my amazing beta readers - Rebekah, Ryan, and my mum. Your input and advice were invaluable. You helped me make this book the best it could be.

Also thank you to Sophie and Ruth for believing in me, and this book.

Most of all, thank you to Gaz, for reminding me what happy feels like. I love you!

Special thanks to Rachel Hollis and Dave Hollis. Neither of them know I exist, but without their daily livestreams, motivational posts and Rachel's book, Girl Wash Your Face, this book would probably still be on my computer and not out in the world.

Shout out to the #authortube community for inspiring me to finish this book. Special thanks go to, Kristen Martin, Vivien Reis, Jenna Moreci, Kim Chance, Natalia Leigh, Mandi Lynn, Mari Suggs, Anna Vera and Bethany Atazadeh. Although I don't know you personally, you all gave me the push I needed to complete this book. Thank you!

Huge gratitude also goes to Joanna Penn. Again, she doesn't know me but her YouTube videos, podcast and website gave me the tools I needed to publish this book. If you don't know who she is and you want to make a living from your writing go to her website www.thecreativepenn.com and also become a patron of hers on Patreon, you won't be disappointed.

If you have read this book because you are in the midst of depression, you are not alone and never will be! More people than you know feel the way you do, including me. Never be too scared to reach out. We are all in it together.

Tell someone how you are feeling. Talking helps.

Natalie x

www.ingramcontent.com/pod-product-compliance
Lightning Source LLC
Chambersburg PA
CBHW062203280526
45788CB00001B/418